Dear Non-Lefty,

The 60 most appalling Lefties

The purpose of this book is purely educational and has been written with a deep and heartfelt Lefty contempt. In it, you will find a by no-means exhaustive list of who I think are the 60 most appalling Lefties – a sort of Lefties Master Class. Originally, I had thought to include the Top 50, but unfortunately there are just too many worthy offenders to miss out.

Lefties come in all shapes and sizes and are pretty much appalling whatever form they take: those who suck-up to Saddam; single-issue Lefties who bang on about one cause at every opportunity, no matter how inappropriate; self-important and pretend Lefties who are only in it for the limelight, and probably the most odious of all – the huge ego Lefties who think they know what's best for the rest of us little people.

At the end of the day this is my list, and I'm sure you've got your own to add to it.

To really get to the bottom of who tops the list of Most Appalling Lefties, please log on to www.mostappallinglefties.com and tell the world who you think should be in the Top 5.

Remember – Baiting Lefties is not a sport that depends on whether or not they are in power. It's a way of life.

Yours, with utter contempt for the bastards.

Richard Thoburn

LEFTIES

*Max***Clifford**
"An unusually hollow, sanctimonious and chippy man."
"The sewer, rather than the sewage."
The Daily Telegraph
Odious.

*Lord***Irvine of Lairg**
The personification of pomposity and self-importance with an expensive taste in wallpaper.

*Sir***Alex Ferguson**
Once a hard-Left shop steward in Govan, a staunch New Labour man now. Bullies have long felt at home in the Labour Party.

IF YOU ARE GOOD AT CHOOSING FOOTBALL TEAMS, APOLOGISING SELLING GOSSIP TO THE TABLOID ARE IN THE SUPER LEAGUE

*George***Galloway**

"Sir, I salute your courage, your strength, your indefatigability."
Every picture tells a story. This one needs no elaboration.

*Ken***Livingstone**

Red Ken is Chairman of the Veronica Wadley fan club and is a friend of Associated Newspapers. Although the holder of high office, he is never too grand to apologise.

EXPENSIVE WALLPAPER, PICKING
SUCKING-UP TO DICTATORS OR
... THE CHANCES ARE THAT YOU
OF VAIN MEGA EGO LEFTIES

LEFTIES

Melvyn **Bragg**

Prolific novelist, screenwriter and broadcaster, has worked for the BBC and LWT, written two-dozen plus books, become Chancellor of Leeds University and for years, has presented radio shows including "Start the Week". A personal friend of Tony Blair, Bragg became Lord Bragg in 1998, but slipped up when he dropped that the Prime Minister was planning on resigning. A Labour party defender of fox hunting, Lord Bragg juggles his rural Cumbrian roots with a modern London lifestyle.

Helen **Mirren**

"Capitalism", Dame Helen told the Guardian "is about pure greed and f*** the others". Lefty actress long based in the US, presumably living in poverty.

Ken **Follett**

Best-selling Lefty novelist, married to Labour MP Barbara, but he has fallen out of love with Tony who he says, will be remembered as the man who made "malicious gossip an everyday tool of British Government".

LUVVIE LEFTIES & NEW
LEFTIES & NEW LABOUR
& NEW LABOUR ME TOO

*Ben***Elton**

Writing comedy for years – stand-up sketches, TV sit-coms, screenplays, novels. His quick-fire wit has very often been directed at the expense of Conservatives, particularly Lady Thatcher. Blackadder, The Thin Blue Line and Friday Night Live also number among his achievements. Staunch Labour-supporter.

*Salman***Rushdie**

In 1989 Ayatollah Khomeini issued a Fatwa on Salman Rushdie. Rugby and Cambridge educated Rushdie often described the UK & US as racist police states but was happy for millions of tax payers' money to be spent on his protection.

LABOUR ME TOO LUVVIE
ME TOO LUVVIE LEFTIES
LUVVIE LEFTIES & NEW

MEDIA LEFTIES

Andrew **Marr**

Started out on the Scotsman, but soon rose up the ranks to become editor of the Independent. He's also worked for the populist Express and the Lefty Observer. As a columnist he called himself centre-left, and while a student at Cambridge, Marr claims he spent much of his time "on marches supporting an (ungrateful) working class". Now the anchor of the BBC's politics coverage.

Clive **Anderson**

Comedian, TV & Radio presenter. When he and Tony Blair were practicing barristers they often played bridge together. Sharp and quick-witted, he regularly makes the guest list at Chequers.

Alan **Rusbridger**

A long-time stalwart of lefty journalism, joined the Guardian in 1979 and is now its editor in chief, even winning the "What the Papers Say" Editor of the Year award in 2001.

Andrew **Rawnlsey**

Chief political columnist of the Observer. Known to Radio 4 listeners as the regular presenter of the Westminster Hour. Rawnsley's book "Servants of the People", is a critical investigation of Blair's first term as PM and highlights the rivalry between Tony and Gordon.

MICROMANAGIN POSITIVEDISCRIMINATI
BUREAUCRATLOVIN MEDDLIN HIGHTAXI
OVERGOVERNIN INTERFERIN RESOURCEWA

*Trevor***Beattie**

Labour Party advertising guru Trevor Beattie is the man behind the "Hello Boys" Wonderbra ads and French Connection's "FCUK" campaign. That's not to mention a portfolio of anti-Tory billboard posters. A formidable ego, Beattie is the only adman to employ his own PR agent. "It seems old-fashioned to talk about class and socialism," he once said, "but I like the words." He can afford to.

*John***Pilger**

Australian born radical Lefty hack who often writes for the Mirror. Pilger labels Blair's government "extreme right wing", and enjoys denouncing "American imperialism" to huddles of students skipping their latest social anthropology lectures. Creative conspiracy theorist.

*James***Naughtie**

Scottish journalist, educated in Aberdeen and New York. Left the staff of the Washington Post in the 1980s to join the Guardian as chief political editor. Naughtie then moved to what has been called the Guardian of the airwaves - the BBC, where he is a presenter on Radio 4.

Gave the game away while interviewing former economic adviser to Gordon Brown, Ed Balls: Naughtie said "when WE win the next election..." This is hardly a surprise, but even Radio 4 Today presenters are not usually so overt.

GOTRIPPIN LEGISLATIN GUARDIANREADIN QUANGOCREATIN DE-MOTIVATIN BIGSPENDIN IN CHAMPAGNESWILLIN APPALLIN LEFTIES

★ LEFTIES

DULL HUMOURLESS WIMMIN

Patricia**Hewitt**

One of Blair's original babes she is responsible for the DTI and is Minister of Wimmin. She entered Parliament with a history in high-level Lefty politics, served as Kinnock's press secretary and co-wrote his famous 'Militant' bashing conference speech.

Cherie**Blair**

She's every bit as nice as she looks… ask Piers Morgan.

Glenda**Jackson**

Great Actress. Lousy politician, albeit one with an independent mind. Not a bundle of laughs… should have stuck to the day job.

IF YOU SPEND ALL YOUR TIME RIGHTS, INEQUALITY AND IT DOES FUNNY THINGS

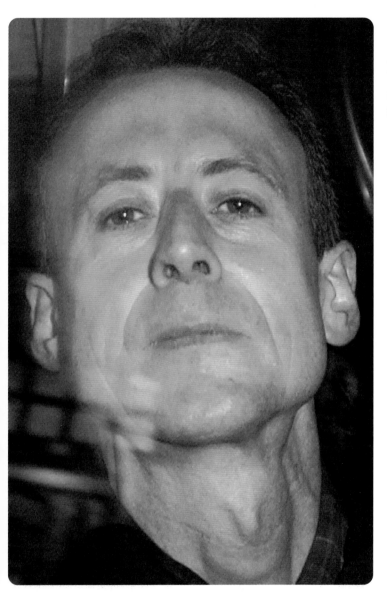

Peter **Tatchell**

The ultimate single issue bore. Managed to lose a safe Labour seat in 1983 by 10,000 votes. Should have stayed in Australia.

Clare **Short**

Robin Cook showed us how to resign with dignity. Clare Short didn't.

Bea **Campbell**

Like Tatchell, another single issue Gay bore, but at least she was smart enough not to stand for election. Sees gender and sexuality issues everywhere. Yawn.

GETTING INDIGNANT OVER GAY POLITICAL CORRECTNESS TO THE WAY YOU LOOK

LEFTIES

CLASS WARRIORS & DINOSAUR

Tony **Benn**

Loony Lefty toff. Re-positioned himself in retirement
as kindly Lefty grandfather. Gave the game away
when being interviewed with an 18 year old Iraqi girl
who was in favour of the war. He's not at all nice.
Vicious, would be authoritarian hard-line Leftist.

Dennis **Skinner**

Occasionally funny, consistently dreadful.
A champion of the proletarian wing of the class
warrior brigade. An anachronistic novelty.

Bruce **Kent**

Unpleasant Soviet apologist/peacenik who used his
dog-collar to pretend he was more than just another
rabid anti-American (public school) Lefty.

TO SECURE FOR ALL THE WORKERS BY HAN
INDUSTRY AND THE MOST EQUITABLE DIST
UPON THE BASIS OF THE COMMON OW
DISTRIBUTION AND EXCHANGE, AND TH
ADMINISTRATION AND CONTROL OF E

Arthur **Scargill**

The ultimate class warrior. Fond of using hordes of miners to intimidate. Egotistical bully who was brought down to earth by Thatcher and was never of any consequence again.

Vanessa **Redgrave**

Child of privilege – part of an acting/theatrical dynasty. Took the loony-Lefty line on just about every issue, alongside less talented but equally spoiled brother Corin.

OR BY BRAIN THE FULL FRUITS OF THEIR
BUTION THEREOF THAT MAY BE POSSIBLE
RSHIP OF THE MEANS OF PRODUCTION,
EST OBTAINABLE SYSTEM OF POPULAR
CH INDUSTRY OF SERVICE. CLAUSE 4.

LEFTIES *(WHO ARE GIRLS)*

*Baroness***Jay**
Daughter of former Labour Prime Minister James Callaghan. Formerly Labour leader of the House of Lords.

*Lady***Antonia Fraser**
Daughter of Lord and Lady Longford, was married to Sir Hugh Fraser and now playwright Harold Pinter. Grand, privileged Lefty writer.

*Fiona***McTaggart**
Parliamentary Under-Secretary of State for Race Equality, Community Policy and Civil Renewal. Her father, Ian McTaggart, was a baronet, a Tory, a eurosceptic and a millionaire.

*Baroness***Mallalieu**
Proof that not all toffs are Tories. A life long member of the Labour party who led the campaign against the ban on fox hunting as President of the Countryside Alliance.

LADY ANTONIA FRASER VI
BARONESS JAY LADY SHAU
MALLALIEU BAB

*Shaun***Woodward**

Crossed the floor to the Labour Party and now represents St. Helens. Used the standard "I didn't leave my party, my party left me" excuse, but wouldn't call a by-election. Married an heiress. Has a butler. Supports fox hunting. Appalling.

*Baroness***Kennedy QC**

QC since '91 and House of Lords since '97. No great fan of Blair these days.

RY RICH FIONA MCTAGGART
N WOODWARD BARONESS
ONESS KENNEDY

LEFTIES *(WHO ARE DEFINITELY NOT GRAND)*

John **"Rocky" Prescott**

When words fail him "Two Jags" has a tendency to resort to his left hook. Lefty-Baiter Nicholas Soames should tread carefully next time he asks the chippy former cruise ship steward for a large Gin & Tonic.

Jeremy **Corbyn**

You can read his rants in The Morning Star. Corbyn is one of the few surviving species of old-school CND Loony Lefties. He still hits the megaphones at Anti-War rallies.

THE WORKERS' FLAG IS DEEPEST RED
DEAD; AND ERE THEIR LIMBS GREW
DYED ITS EVERY FOLD. THEN RAIS
BENEATH ITS FOLDS WE'LL LIVE A
AND TRAITORS SNEER. WE'LL KI

*John***Reid**

Tough talking Scot and transient Lefty minister. A Blairite loyalist who managed to clock up four different cabinet jobs in the space of a year. At the moment he's Secretary of State for Health, but he's tried his hand at Transport, Leader of the House of Commons, Scottish Secretary and Northern Ireland Secretary. The "attack dog" seems to have become a little sensitive about his accent lately, if a recent interview with Paxman was anything to go by.

*Michael***"Gorbals Mick"Martin**

The Speaker of the House of Commons probably talks a great deal of sense.

And when simultaneous translation is introduced we will all be much better informed.

T SHROUDED OFT OUR MARTYRED
STIFF AND COLD THEIR LIFE-BLOOD
E THE SCARLET STANDARD HIGH:
D DIE, THOUGH COWARDS FLINCH
P THE RED FLAG FLYING HERE

LEFTIES

POMPOUS SELF-IMPORTANT LEGAL

*Lord***Irvine of Lairg**

"It's time for young Blair to bring us whisky" was an over-used line during his visits to Chequers and his former pupil eventually tired of his grand ways.

*Lord***Falconer**

The ultimate Tony's crony, Charlie Falconer and the PM go back a long way. They knew each other at school and shared a flat together when they were junior barristers and still into rock music. Tony appointed his old friend to the Lords in 1997 and Falconer soon stepped into government. The Dome is only one of his many successes.

MICROMANAGIN POSITIVEDISCRIMINATI
BUREAUCRATLOVIN MEDDLIN HIGHTAXI
OVERGOVERNIN INTERFERIN RESOURCEWA

*Michael***Mansfield QC**

'Moneybags' Mansfield laps up the media spotlight and is known for defending the indefensible, opposing the monarchy, espousing socialism despite a Tory upbringing, and sipping champagne. Famous for liking a bit of flesh in some senses but not others, Moneybags likes the ladies but is also a vegetarian.

*Baroness***Kennedy QC**

Baroness Kennedy, the 'nation's favourite Portia' apparently. Top barrister, defender of just causes, head of the multi-million pound, Foreign Office-funded British Council. An interesting choice considering her alleged past sympathies for the International Association of Democratic Lawyers, a Soviet front organisation.

GOTRIPPIN LEGISLATIN GUARDIANREADIN QUANGOCREATIN DE-MOTIVATIN BIGSPENDIN IN CHAMPAGNESWILLIN APPALLIN LEFTIES

CONTROL-FREAK PSYCHO

*Gordon*Brown

The longest continuous serving Chancellor of the Exchequer since Gladstone, Brown has worked hard at cultivating an image of prudence in economic management, in spite of the plethora of 'stealth taxes'. Each budget reinforces his reputation as a complexifier rather than a simplifier, as the temptation to meddle and micro-manage always proves irresistible. He is storing up trouble with his extravagant public spending... but the pigeons will not come home to roost until the next Parliament. In the meantime the brooding resentment at Blair not giving way for him to take over the leadership will be put on hold until after the election. Could teach Claudio Ranieri a thing or two about 'tinkering'.

ALASTAIR HATES PETER GORD
TONY ALASTAIR HATES GORD
PETER HATES ALASTAIR
ALASTAIR LOVES TONY PETER H

Y FLAWED)

PEOPLE

*Peter***Mandelson**

The epitome of New Labour, Mandy was once briefly a member of the Young Communist League. He worked in television and PR before being elected as Labour MP for Hartlepool, a far cry from his metropolitan lifestyle in the South. So alien is this Northern working-class constituency, that Mandy reportedly asked for the guacamole dip in a fish and chip shop, only to be told it was mushy peas. His devotion to Blair did not save him from twice having to resign from the Cabinet but it certainly helped him make a spectacular return to the corridors of power as the EU's Trade Commissioner.

*Alastair***Campbell**

Likes to play the hard man with a hint of menace. For example, this is what he had to say on February 7th 2005:

"Peter Mandelson did a good job on the Today programme, warning the BBC not to resume their demonisation of me. They need to leave me alone and concentrate on the important issues. **Because we all know what happened before."**

ON HATES TONY PETER LOVES
ON CHARLIE LOVES GORDON
GORDON HATES ALASTAIR
ES GORDON TONY LOVES TONY

POSH

LEFTIES *(WHO WOULD RATHER YOU DIDN'T KNOW WHERE THEY WENT TO SCHOOL)*

*Ruth***Kelly**

Not only was Ruth Kelly the youngest woman ever to sit in the Cabinet, but she has given birth to more children in office than any other MP ever. Kelly, schooled in economics at Oxford, LSE and the Guardian. She seems shy about acknowledging that she attended Westminster School. Perhaps with this background, she won't make a school dinner out of her education post.

*Harriet***Harman**

St. Pauls educated Harriet Harman has been a Labour front-bencher since the early 1980s. As Blair's first social security secretary she stepped down very soon after clashes with fellow minister Frank Field only to return to the Cabinet in 2001 as Solicitor General.

ETON WESTMINSTER
COLLEGE SHERBOURNE ST

*Mark***Fisher**

A Labour back-bencher who was once a playwright and author but now plays the part of a relatively regular dissenter from the party line. Eton-educated one-time Arts Minister.

*Hugh***Hudson**

This British film director has spent much of his life apologising for his Eton education. The 1981 "Chariots of Fire" was created to be a radical condemnation of Establishment elitism and privilege. Unfortunately for him many took it as a celebration of the Thatcherite values of the '80s. Perhaps people also got the wrong end of the stick after watching his party election broadcast for Neil Kinnock: it was supposed to make them vote *for* the Labour party.

*Rosie***Boycott**

Rosie has edited rags as diverse as the Express and the Independent and has appeared on numerous dumbed-down TV shows as well as an embarrassing TV campaign for the Express. As Britain's first female broadsheet editor, she famously advocated the decriminalisation of cannabis. Educated at that bastion of Socialism, Cheltenham Ladies College.

*Tam***Dalyell**

The Father of the House and Labour party long-timer Tam Dalyell is also a hereditary baronet. Sir Tam must be the only member of the hard-left Campaign Group to have a peacock collection at his country house. A shabby Old Etonian.

CHELTENHAM LADIES
AUL'S TRINITY COLLEGE ETON

DULL EARNEST GREY BORING

*John***Birt**

Director General of the BBC until 2000, Liverpudlian Birt has spent a long time in the media. At London Weekend Television in the 1970's he employed Peter Mandelson as a researcher. Made a Life Peer in 1999, Lord Birt has worked more recently as part-time unpaid adviser to the Prime Minister. Bundle of laughs.

*Trevor***Phillips**

Trevor Phillips OBE challenged Frank Dobson for the Labour nomination in the race to be the first London Mayor. He lost that but became Dobbo's running mate. It goes without saying that the pair didn't quite make it, but Phillips has every intention of becoming Mayor one day. The former leader of the National Union of Students is now Chair of the Commission for Racial Equality and has been Chair of the new London Assembly.

STRAW, CLARKE, AND PHILLIPS ARE ALL
UNION OF STUDENTS. FOR ALL THEIR
MEETINGS, BECOMING INDIGNANT, PASS
OF US WHAT WE SHOULD BE DOING
BIRT DEVELOPED HIS OWN UNIQUE

*Jack***Straw** – **Letting his hair down**

With a hard Left past, Straw first came to public prominence in the late 1960's as leader of the National Union of Students. Became Home Secretary and later Foreign Secretary. He rang out the New Labour theme of "tough on crime, tough on the causes of crime", and famously condemned "aggressive beggars, winos and squeegee merchants".

*Charles***Clarke**

Esteemed Toby jug impersonator, favours picking up his top jobs on the back of other people's fallouts… Estelle, David. First joined the Cabinet in 2001 in a constitutionally shady role as Chairman of the Labour Party. Labour already had an elected party Chairman at the time, but, hey, what are a few constitutional rules set in stone amongst New Labour friends?

ORMER PRESIDENTS OF THE NATIONAL
DULT LIVES THEY HAVE BEEN ATTENDING
G RESOLUTIONS AND TELLING THE REST
F WE WERE AS WISE AS THEY ARE.
AND OF CHARISMA ALL ON HIS OWN.

LEFTIES *(WHO WEAR THEIR CLUBS ON THEIR SLEEVE)*

*Alastair***Campbell - Burnley**

A household name - curious for a press secretary - he became Blair's de facto Minister For Spin in 1994. Campbell's early career included a stint writing erotic stories for an adult magazine before moving on to more mainstream journalism. Blair described Campbell bluntly as a "reformed drunk" to Vladimir Putin, but it's usually Campbell being direct. When asked about the PM's religion, Campbell replied: "We don't do God. I'm sorry. We don't do God."

Brash and hard-hitting, Campbell resigned in 2003 to get his "life back", but he is back in the saddle for the election campaign. Famed for his polite text messages, easy-going nature and all round good humour.

*Charlie***Whelan - Spurs**

An all round pint-swilling, Spurs supporting, piss-taking baiter of Mandy and Campbell and general good lad. Charlie is charismatic with a great sense of humour. The only problem is if someone mentions Gordon. Charlie - has anyone ever told you that naked hero-worship by one middle-aged man for another is seriously uncool?

PORTRAYING YOURSELF AS A
EASIER TO SOME THAN TO OT
SO LONG AS YOU DON'T MEI
WORK A BIT HARDER. ALL OF THI
TO PROMOTE THEIR LOVE

*Tony***Banks – Chelsea**

Left winger, briefly Sports Minister and one-time Chairman of the Greater London Council. Failed to get the Labour nomination for London Mayor in the first mayoral election. Unlike Kate Hoey, another ill-fated Sports Minister, he is passionately against hunting. Apparently fishing is OK though, because it's popular with Labour voters.
A deep thinker who once likened William Hague to a 'foetus'.

*Greg***Dyke – Manchester United**

The Labour party can thank him for generous donations, the rest of us can thank him for Roland Rat. This former Director General of the BBC was pushed to resign from the position after the Hutton Inquiry condemned his organisation for slapdash reporting over the Iraq war. A life-long supporter of Manchester United, where he sat on the board prior to joining the BBC.

MAN OF THE PEOPLE COMES
HERS. CHARLIE IS A NATURAL
TION GORDON. TONY HAS TO
HAVE DECIDED IT'S EXPEDIENT
OF THE BEAUTIFUL GAME.

Chris **Martin**

Lead singer of pop band Coldplay, Chris Martin's aim in life is to graduate from "third-rate Bono" to "a full-on Bono", by which he means as a campaigner for a medley of Lefty causes. The name of his daughter, Apple, tells you all you need to know. Crusading for "fair trade" and against globalisation, Martin has promoted petitions and campaigns.

Mick **Hucknall**

Multimillionaire frontman for Simply Red, has always associated himself with centre-left politics. He's been known to attend Alan Milburn's champagne receptions, pep talks from Tony Blair, not to mention funding the Labour party. Told the New Statesman he might even consider standing for Parliament one day.

SUCCESS IN SHOW BUSINESS
CONFERS PROFOUND
WHICH THESE DEEP TH

*Chris***Evans**

Another whining ginger Lefty northerner. A generous supporter of Red Ken in his battle against Frank Dobson to be Mayor of London.

*Paul***Weller**

Lead singer of The Jam and later the Style Council, famed for the pretentious sleeve notes on his albums and anti-capitalist rants.

*Miss***Dynamite**

Niomi McLean-Daley was the first black female performer to win the Mercury Music prize. She is often known to switch the microphone for the megaphone as she preaches against the government at leftwing rallies. "I don't feel that there's anyone in the cabinet at all that I can relate to", she told Newsnight, and rumour has it that she's looking for a career in politics.

AND MUSIC AUTOMATICALLY POLITICAL WISDOM NKERS WANT TO SHARE

LEFTIES *(THE MOST APPALLING COUPLES)*

Neil **&** *Glenys***Kinnock**

When the Welsh windbag finally realised he'd never win power in Britain he packed his bags and loitered around until he was sent off to Brussels as a Commissioner. His wife Glenys joined him in Europe as an MEP for Wales. The two are said to be seen roaming around the Continent straightening bananas and reddening tape.

*Harriet***Harman &** *Jack***Dromey**

Posh Harriet is married to prole former Grunwick picket leader Jack Dromey. He's challenged Bill Morris as leader of the TGWU with the slogan "New Labour, New T & G". Lost. She has done a better job of walking the tightrope between Blair & Brown.

Ken **&** *Barbara***Follett**

Ken and Barbie are the ultimate champagne socialist couple. In the mid-1990's Barbara, MP for Stevenage, gained a reputation as the Labour Party's unofficial 'image consultant', advising the male (and maybe some of the female) MPs to be less hairy. Ken's a multimillionaire novelist and likes a good glass of bubbly most nights, apparently.

REALLY APPALLING LEFTIES WILL ONL

INBREEDING

Tony **&** Cherie**Blair**

The Prime Minister, perhaps history's most image-obsessed leader, is attacked for political spin, smarm and selling out. Known for surrounding himself with Tony's Cronies, Blair Babes, Big Businesses and Peter Mandelson, he still found time to have a child while in office. Wife and fellow barrister Cherie always insists on the name 'Booth' – except on speaking tours, when 'Blair' is no doubt much more lucrative. The PM has been close with both Presidents Clinton and Bush. Some say power goes to his head, and he's certainly had more of it than any Labour leader before him.

Bill **&** Hillary**Clinton**

Perhaps 'merger' defines this collaboration between ambitious politicians better than 'marriage'. He was popular when he left office, not least with chum Tony Blair. Wife Hillary is now Senator for New York and many predict she'll run for the White House in 2008 – if the "vast rightwing conspiracy" hasn't snuffed her chances by then. She threw her weight around plenty as non-elected first Lady. But that will be nothing compared to the horrors that will be unleashed if the politically correct one makes it to the White House in her own right.

Chris**Martin** **&** Gwyneth**Paltrow**

"I think George Bush is such an embarrassment to America", the Hollywood actress has declared. Her Democratic-leanings have manifested themselves in donations to the John Kerry campaign for the presidency as well as hand-outs to other political groups. The Oscar prize-winner is married to popstar Brit Chris Martin and the pair never cease to make a song and dance about exploitation by the rich world of the poor. Paltrow's said she worries about bringing up a child in America – but British state-owned hospitals were evidently not a suitable alternative for the birth of her daughter.

MARRY FROM THEIR OWN TRIBE AND
IS COMMON

LEFTIES

*Adair***Turner**

When Adair Turner was director general of the CBI, plenty of businessmen thought that the CBI was far too friendly to ministers. Turner is now a senior Downing Street adviser.

*Chris***Patten**

A lifelong Tory and former Party Chairman, Patten is a chum of Tony Blair and much mistrusted among rightwingers in England. Having lost his seat he went on to oversee the handover of Hong Kong to China and, in the eyes of many, of Britain to Brussels.

FOR SOME, PROXIMITY TO POWER IS A F
PRINCIPLE. BLAIR MAGIC WHEN APPLIE
GAVE A WHOLE NEW MEAN

*George***Cox**

Does anyone remember the Institute of Directors (IoD)? They used to be a forthright defender of business and free market principles. No more. In Ruth Lea, the IoD's former head of policy, they had a highly effective public face which was not popular with New Labour.

George Cox, former director-general, has successfully emasculated the IoD by pursuing a policy of collaboration with the Government. Ruth Lea was fired and Cox is alleged to have persuaded Lord Young to stand down as IoD president.

Cox is currently Chairman of the Design Council. He is leading a review, announced by Chancellor Brown in his 2005 Budget, into how creativity can help businesses perform better.

Is it really part of the role of Government to tell businesses how to use creativity and design?

MORE POTENT FORCE THAN POLITICAL
O SOME MIDDLE-AGED CONSERVATIVES
G TO THE TERM 'GROUPIE'.

LEFTIES *(LIMOUSINE LIBERALS)*

*Michael***Moore**

Producer of leftwing documentaries, author of leftwing books, and one-time editor of leftwing political magazine Mother Jones. His Fahrenheit 9/11 won a Cannes Film Festival award, and when Bowling for Columbine won an Oscar, Moore spouted a rant against George Bush in his acceptance speech. Not as nice as he looks.

*Susan***Sarandon**

Esteemed film actress and card-carrying member of Hollywood's Lefty Elite. Sarandon, whose life partner is the equally worthy Tim Robbins, has tiresomely used her Hollywood status to stand up and defend the value of her free speech rights and Lefty principles.

More recently Sarandon has been perfecting her role as acclaimed Bush-hater and anti-war campaigner. In one of her more famous quotes she noted: "You're so lucky in Ireland, England and Spain. Everyone there already knows what it's like to have inexplicable terrorist violence."

BUSH HATIN LIMO RIDIN LIMELIGH
SADDAM JUSTIFYIN CONSPIRACY WEAVIN P
LEGISLATIN MEDDLIN OVERGOVERNIN INT

Senator **Ted Kennedy**
Fighting for working Americans

Ah, good old longstanding Lefty Senator Ted; noble champion of Worthy Causes. Elected to Senate in 1962, Ted Kennedy has dedicated much time and effort to emanating the very beat of the heart of progressive Democratic politics. From meals on wheels, to civil rights, to cleaner water to the minimum wage, Senator Ted's your man. The very pillar of a true and just Democratic society.

Lest we forget Chappaquiddick, Senator. Or the time when you ran away from your studies at Harvard and hired someone to take your exam, or that time when you ran away from the police during a speeding incident in Virginia, or that time you left your wife?

Hillary **Clinton**

Is Hillary Rodham hoping to be America's First Elected Iron Lady? Well, she spent 8 years unofficially in the role. Some say she's the real tour de force in the Clinton political partnership. And was it Hillary in the back row who was seen breathing a sigh of relief when Kerry was out-voted by Dubya?

Barbra **Streisand**

The New York-born American singer, movie star, producer and director personifies Hollywood limousine liberalism. Streisand is known for her outspoken Lefty views. She came out in favour of Senator Kerry in 2004, pushes for environmentalist action, and has always backed the Democrats. "I am simple, complex, generous, selfish, unattractive, beautiful, lazy, and driven", is how she once described herself.

GRABBIN MORALISIN TAX 'N SPENDIN
ETIN POSITIVEDISCRIMINATIN EGOTRIPPIN
FERIN RESOURCEWASTIN APPALLIN LEFTIES

Appendix IV **MOST APPALLING**

Gadaffi

Castro

Chavez

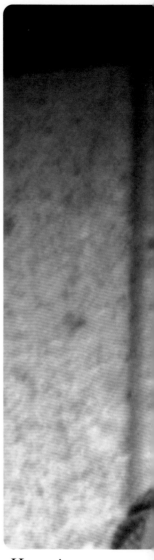

Hussein

APART FROM A TOTAL INTOLERANCE OF D
A PERSONAL VANITY THAT KNOWS NO BO
ON END, A HABIT OF PLASTERING THEI
TENDENCY TO LIVE IN THE LAP OF LUXUR
MASSES, WHAT DO THESE CHARMERS HAV

Mugabe

Putin

SENT, DISREGARD FOR THE RULE OF LAW,
DS, AN ABILITY TO DRONE ON FOR HOURS
ICTURES ALL OVER THE PLACE AND A
HILE CLAIMING TO BE AT ONE WITH THE
COMMON? YES... THEY ARE ALL LEFTIES.

With thanks to all the [_____] I have baited during my life, and all the [_____] who have worked with me on this project. It's truly wonderful to see what [_____] will do for money.